Watch it Grow

A Sunflower's Life

Nancy Dickmann

www.raintreepublishers.co.uk
Visit our website to find out
more information about
Raintree books.

To order:
☎ Phone 0845 6044371
🖨 Fax +44 (0) 1865 312263
✉ Email myorders@raintreepublishers.co.uk

Customers from outside the UK please telephone +44 1865 312262

Raintree is an imprint of Capstone Global Library Limited,
a company incorporated in England and Wales having its
registered office at 7 Pilgrim Street, London, EC4V 6LB
– Registered company number: 6695582

Text © Capstone Global Library Limited 2010
First published in hardback in 2010
The moral rights of the proprietor have been asserted

...ced in
...it in any
...r incidentally
...nission of
...of the
...f a licence
...) Kirby Street,
...ight owner's

...eitch

ISBN 978 0 431 19541 4
14 13 12 11 10
10 9 8 7 6 5 4 3 2 1

British Library Cataloguing in Publication Data
Dickmann, Nancy.
Sunflower. -- (Watch it grow)
583.9'9-dc22

Acknowledgements
We would would like to thank the following for permission to reproduce
photographs: iStockphoto pp. **4** (© Daniel MAR), **6** (© Feng Yu), **8**
(© moshimochi), **9** (© Terje Borud), **11** (© Mary Bustraan), **13** (yellowiris),
16 (© ra-photos), **17** (© Andrey Stratilatov), **18** (© Kathy Dewar),
19 (© Ints Vikmanis), **20** (© Yuri Maryunin), **21** (© LyaC), **22 right**
(© Mary Bustraan), **22 top** (© Feng Yu), **22 left** (© ra-photos), **23 middle
top** (Arlindo 71), **23 middle bottom** (© Terje Borud); Photolibrary p. **12**
(Garden Picture Library/© Kate Gadsby); Shutterstock pp. **5** (© irin-K),
7 (CamPot), **10** (© Evon Lim Seo Ling), **14** (© Tropinina Olga), **15**
(© kukuruxa), **22 bottom** (© Tropinina Olga), **23 bottom** (© Evon Lim
Seo Ling), **23 top** (© Tropinina Olga).

Front cover photograph (main) of a field of sunflowers reproduced with
permission of iStockphoto (ooyoo). Front cover photograph (inset) of a
close-up of sunflower seeds reproduced with permission of Shutterstock
(© BW Folsom). Back cover photograph of a sunflower shoot reproduced
with permission of iStockphoto (© Mary Bustraan).

The publisher would like to thank Nancy Harris for her assistance in the
preparation of this book.

Every effort has been made to contact copyright holders of material
reproduced in this book. Any omissions will be rectified in subsequent
printings if notice is given to the publisher.

Contents

Life cycles

All living things have a life cycle.

A sunflower has a life cycle.

seed

A sunflower starts as a tiny seed.

The seed grows into a sunflower.
Later it will die.

Seeds and shoots

A sunflower seed grows in
the ground.

root

Roots grow down from the seed into the ground.

shoot

A shoot grows from the seed.

leaves

Leaves grow from the shoot.

Becoming a flower

The sunflower plant needs water and sunlight to grow.

The sunflower plant grows taller.

bud

A bud grows at the top of the plant.

petals

The bud opens. There are yellow
petals inside.

Making seeds

The flower turns towards the sun.

A bee comes to feed on the flower.
The bee has pollen on it.

new seeds

The pollen helps make new sunflower seeds grow in the flower.

The flower dies.

Some seeds fall to the ground.

The life cycle starts again.

Life cycle of a sunflower

1 A sunflower seed grows in the ground.

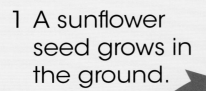

2 A shoot and leaves grow from the seed.

4 The bud opens into a sunflower.

3 A bud grows at the top of the plant.

Picture glossary

bud part of a plant that opens into a flower

pollen yellow powder inside a flower

root part of a plant that grows underground. Roots take up water for the plant to use.

shoot small green stem that grows from a seed

Index

Notes to parents and teachers

Before reading

Ask the children if they have ever grown flowers. Ask them if they know what a plant needs to grow. Show them some sunflower seeds. What else do they know that grows from seeds?

After reading

- Put the children into groups and give them three yogurt pots, some soil, and three sunflower seeds. Show them how to plant the seeds and label the pots 1, 2, and 3. Tell them to put pot 1 in sunlight and water it every day, to put pot 2 in sunlight but give it no water, and to put pot 3 in a dark place away from sunlight and water it every day. Ask them to keep a record of what happens to their seeds. Ask them which seed did best. Why do they think this happened and what can they conclude about plants' needs?

- Tell the children that seeds are a good energy food. Roast some sunflower seeds and eat them together as a healthy snack.